MAKING MUSIC: 25 MOTIVATIONAL CREATIVITY TIPS FOR
ELECTRONIC MUSIC PRODUCTION

ROY WILKENFELD

What Is This Book?

Making Music: 25 Motivational Creativity Tips for Electronic Music Production is a handbook about creative methods and practices in music production, spanning over five different categories. These five categories are: The Beginning, Sound Design, Arrangement, Songwriting and Motivation.

Making Music discusses important issues concerning the music production process, taking the reader through all vital steps of music production in a helpful and inspiring way. The book offers fresh, practical ideas and new perspectives to approach each step of music production with.

The first chapter, *The Beginning*, is aimed to help music producers in the process of finding the right path and mood to get a new track started, without fighting a creative block.

The second chapter, *Sound Design*, explains methods to diversify and revive your sound design efforts to have the best sounds possible ready for your next piece of music.

The third chapter, *Arrangement*, includes concrete methods and perspectives to approach music arrangement with.

The fourth chapter, *Songwriting*, talks about songwriting practices and inspiration to get the best out of you musically. The chapter includes methods to write music.

The fifth and final chapter, *Motivation*, includes useful motivational tips that musicians can never get enough of, enabling you to get the best out of yourself spiritually and maximize your music production efforts.

While the book is aimed primarily for electronic music producers, the tips and methods are universally applicable for all modern music producers.

How to Use This Book

Making Music can be approached in several ways.

The book can be used as a motivational handbook for musicians and music producers in their long and difficult but rewarding journey in music. The book is a great resort when extra motivation is needed or if the music making spirits are low.

Making Music contains plenty of practical and useful methods of approaching music creation in all of its five categories, which makes the book a perfect match and support for music production sessions, both during and prior to them.

Ideally, the goal of this book is to spark inspiration in any area of music creation, be it the beginning of the music production process, writing a song, arranging music, sound design or just when you looking for that extra inspiration or "tap in the back", so to speak.

It is recommended that you have this book close by during your music making sessions as a quick reference. Making Music will also provide great company while traveling and out of the studio, offering deep and insightful advice about music production.

Page intentionally left blank.

CONTENTS

INTRODUCTION

Making music is a large process that differs from musician to musician, each having their own ways and preferences of getting things done. In this book you will learn about five key areas of music production, most of which likely are already familiar to you but provide fresh and creative perspectives as well as practical methods.

The 25 tips included in this book are supplied together with clear descriptions and necessary tutorials as well as exclusive *Pro Tips* to boost your music production knowledge.

Making Music is designed to help you *make* more music. Think, analyze and further develop the ideas discussed in this book and you'll find yourself making better and more inspirational music than ever.

Have fun Making Music!

-Roy Wilkenfeld

CHAPTER 1 - THE BEGINNING

01 FREE YOUR AGENDA FOR MAKING MUSIC

Getting rid of distractions is vital prior to entering the music making zone.

Right when you are starting to focus in music, you'll receive a phone call from a friend asking to hang out, or a text message which leads to a long chat, or maybe your roommate or partner is constantly invading your precious studio space. Or maybe you have a date planned for later, which leaves you anticipating and thinking about that instead of music. Sounds familiar? Situations like these will ensure that your music making will never truly begin for that day. A few simple, disciplinary home remedies can take care of the situation easily.

How to: Create a private atmosphere for music making sessions

1. Mute or turn off your cell phone and place it out of your reach, the screen facing downwards. This way you'll avoid the audiovisual distractions of the cell phone.

2. Create a sign on your door that says "I'm making music – do not interrupt. Thank you!" Simple, yet effective.

3. Do not plan anything else for the day you decide to make music to achieve a peace of mind of solely making music – and to eventually reach the *zone*. The only way to get into the zone is to devote yourself to making music for a long period of time, staying free of distractions.

4. Have a continuous supply of coffee or tea to keep you focused. Think of the coffee or tea cup as a symbol of making music.

Pro Tip #1: If you have a tight daily schedule, buy a calendar where you'll define the music making hours – and follow them. Set an alarm on your cell phone so you do not need to worry about when to stop. Until the alarm, just immerse yourself in music and try to forget about the rest of your schedule.

Pro Tip #2: Turn off the Internet. Unplug the cable or turn off the router. This is the simplest trick to get rid of the temptations of the Internet.

Chapter 1 The Beginning

In order to make music, you'll need to get in the right kind of mood.

You might have freed your agenda and gotten rid of distractions, but you notice that you're not in the right mood to start making music. This is usual, because lots of things can be on our minds at once, which is no surprise. In order to get in the right mood, there are various methods you can do to find the necessary spark of creativity. These can include physical exercise or listening to relaxing music, for example.

How to: Get struck by the music making mood

1. Go outside for an hour or two, doing something physical, such as your favorite hobby. Even a walk in the park can be effective enough. The fact is, your brain will start working properly when you go outdoors and breathe fresh air, resulting in fresh ideas.

2. Meditate by listening to relaxing music for a short period of time (20-30 minutes), to get your spirits lifted.

3. Listen to some of your favorite artists at a high volume to get hyped and inspired. Also, when you start to make music, keep the volume cranked to *feel* the music.

4. Take care of all your daily matters before diving into music, so you'll know there's nothing else between you and the music. Your mind will stay at ease.

Pro Tip #1: Lighting is important. Set an intimate mood in your room by dimming all lights. Introduce some colored lights to enhance the experience.

Pro Tip #2: Clean your room and sort out your desk. A clean environment will emphasize the "pro"–factor in your music making and will inspire you to take music production seriously, therefore getting in the right mood faster.

Chapter 1 The Beginning

03 WHERE TO START?

The greatest question in creating a piece of music – where to start?

To get your music started is like climbing a hill from its steepest side. But when you get to the top, the descent will be much easier. The difficulties in the process of starting a piece of music can be called a *creative block*. If you feel like nothing is happening, try the following methods to actually get your music going and your productive flow started.

How to: Kickstart your music production process

1. Listen to your favorite track and recreate the same basic drum pattern or groove used in it. You'll start adding your own touches around it in no time and don't have to put too much thought on creating one from scratch.

2. Start by doing sound design. Create a few sounds using synthesizers to spark inspiration. Design a bass sound, pad sound, lead sound and a keyboard sound to use in your track, so they are ready and playable.

3. Play around with your favorite instrument. Play until you find yourself playing a satisfying chord or melody pattern. Continue playing the pattern so you'll memorize it and can use it as the *theme* of the track you're about to make. Have a drum groove playing so you can play melodies to the tempo of the track.

4. Create great kick, clap and hi-hat sounds. Just to put these three together is enough to inspire you into making the rest of the track. The kick, clap and hi-hat are the basic foundation for any dance and pop track when it comes to drums. Sample packs are the easiest route to finding good sounds for drums – such as those made by companies like Wave Alchemy.

Pro Tip #1: There are tons of ways to start making music. You need to find your own way of starting a track and form a routine doing it, so you'll always have a working way to start your music. Approach one track with a specific method (for example: start one with drums and the other with chords) – after you've finished a few tracks you'll know which methods work best for you.

Pro Tip #2: Let technology inspire you. Sometimes getting a new plugin or hardware instrument is essential to get you inspired to make music again. At least download some demos of software instruments and plugins – some developers such as FabFilter offer fully functional 30-day demos.

Chapter 1 The Beginning

8

04 Let the DAW Guide You

Most often than not, you'll be able to make music just by "showing up" to your studio and your DAW.

Open up the DAW (Digital Audio Workstation) every day – and magical things will happen. According to the *80/20 – rule*, by making music every day for ten days, two of those days will result in something absolutely special. Rather than making music once or twice a week for three hours, make music every day for an hour. Just open your DAW and start making something. It's that simple. Your DAW will guide you the rest of the way. Quantity comes over quality, always.

How to: Approach music in different ways in your DAW

1. The *sound design approach*: Start by creating sounds. You could use samples, instruments or synthesizers as your sources for sound design. Apply effects and tweak parameters to mangle sound in different ways. The aim is to create inspiring sounds that you can use to build your track with.

2. The *drum programming approach*: Use your favorite sampler to program drum grooves. Drum programming is one of the easiest methods to get music rolling because it forms the rhythmic foundation. Other elements, such as melodic and harmonic ones can be built around the drum groove.

3. The *melodic approach*: The classic music writing method. Start by improvising on your most natural instrument, such as the piano, guitar, bass or a synthesizer. Create a fairly simple melodic hook or chord progression and build more melodic elements around them to achieve a more complex entity. Drums can be added later, but you can also form the music around the drums.

4. The *copycat approach*: Import your favorite track into your DAW with the project set to the right tempo, same as the track you import. Duplicate the groove, chord progression or other ideas from the track by using your own sounds and methods. Don't go too far with this though. Do "steal" elements from your favorite music with good taste, but don't exercise plagiarism. It's fine to let other music influence your own.

Pro Tip: Put emphasis on sound design. Create sounds in your own peace and feel enthusiastic and experimental about the process. You'll end up with truly unique sounds that will boost your music making to a whole new level. Experiment with uncommon ways of creating sounds. Use out-of-the-ordinary plugins, live recordings, etc.

Chapter 1 The Beginning

05 CREATE A CUSTOM TEMPLATE

One of the best things you can do to yourself as a music producer is create a custom project template.

Can you count how many times you've done the same routines of adding certain plugins, track configurations and routings in your projects? Be smart and make yourself a custom project template that you can use whenever you start a new track. You can make modifications to the template along your music making journey and perfect it throughout the years. The point is to have a ready-made project with all of your favorite settings, instruments, samplers and plugins ready to go and routed, named and colored accordingly. You'll spend hours and hours less monthly and save time for actually *making* music.

How to: Make yourself a custom DAW template

1. Open a fresh, clean project in your DAW.

2. Add your favorite instruments to it so they are instantly playable.

3. Create your favorite effect and plugin chains for the chosen instruments, such as delays and reverbs.

4. Create buses (or submixes) for all drums, music, vocals, basses and other instrument groups. Route all instruments into their correct group buses, then route the submixes to the master bus. By using group buses, you can easily process certain instrument groups as a whole or adjust their relative volumes by using a single fader.

5. Add your favorite plugins on the master bus if needed, such as a compressor, limiter, spectrum analyzer and metering plugins. If you don't need anything on the master, leave it empty.

6. Color-code everything. Make all drums green, basses red, melodic instruments pink, and so on.

6. Make sure the template works and is flawless, and doesn't have anything that's useless. Remember to name everything properly so you'll never have a problem starting a track using the template.

7. Update the template whenever you feel like changing or tweaking something for improvement and save it as a new version. Always include the date in the template (for example: ProductionTemplate_07252015).

Pro Tip: Make different templates for different styles of music and different time signatures. You could have a "Techno Template" and a "Hip Hop Template", among others.

Chapter 1 The Beginning

06 GET FRESH, QUALITY SAMPLES

Quality-sounding samples are the heart of your electronic productions.

Always strive to acquire samples of great quality, because your music will be represented by them, more or less. There are two ways to do it: buy commercial sample packs or record your own samples. Quite a few quality sample companies can be found online, offering great sample packs, especially drums. There is nothing wrong in using commercial samples, but making your own samples is not only rewarding, but absolutely unique. All you need is a microphone. Basically, as a modern producer, you already would own the rest of the necessities, such as a sound card with a microphone input and your DAW to record with. With a decent ($99) microphone, you'll get a high quality, unprocessed sound – just wait until you get to process your samples with plugin compressors, saturators and distortion.

How to: Record your own drum samples in your studio

1. Connect your microphone to your sound card and insert a healthy level of gain from the sound card's preamp to get a clear, audible signal, but make sure not to clip (never go above 0db on your digital meter) the signal. Make sure you get the signal in your DAW as well by choosing the correct microphone input for your mixer channel.

2. Gather anything you might think would make a great sound: pepper and salt shakers, paper, silverware, water in a bottle, or anything else you might think of.

3. Arm a track to record in your DAW and start recording some drum hits, one at a time, leaving a little space between each hit, so the sound have enough time to decay naturally.

4. Listen and browse through your recordings and chop the best bits of drum hits and export them into a new folder (for example: Drums – Shakers and Silverware [July 11 2015]).

5. Import your freshly made drum hits to your favorite sampler to trigger them from – and make music! This is also the step to apply further processing to your samples, using plugins.

Chapter 2 Sound Design

Pro Tip #1: When you hunt for commercial samples, aim for dry and natural-sounding samples and not the ones that are already processed to death and the ones that are already heard on countless of electronic music records. You'll want to stand out from the crowd with your samples.

Pro Tip #2: If you decide to record your own samples, make sure to chop the drum hits in the beginning of the transient, so they'll play out properly and have enough punch.

07 ACQUIRE UNUSUAL SYNTHS AND PLUGINS

The best sources of inspiration in sound design come from unusual instruments and effects processors.

Get your hands on fresh sound design tools such as *granular*, *wavetable* and *FM* (frequency modulation) synthesizers and don't rely on your "basic" *subtractive* synthesizers for the creation of every single sound. Aim to research for unique plugin effects, such as the ones that can modulate pitch, reverse the sound and mangle the input signal in otherworldly ways, normally unable to achieve with bread-and-butter effects such as your regular delay or reverb plugins. Here are a few suggestions of great commercial synthesizers and plugins: Padshop Pro by Steinberg for granular synthesis, XferRecords Serum for wavetable synthesis, Native Instruments FM8 for FM synthesis, Soundtoys Crystallizer for granular reverse echo effects and Valhalla Shimmer for reverbs straight out of a dream world.

Pro Tip #1: Use resampling to your advantage. When you create sounds with synthesizers and plugins, bounce the result to disk and process those files again – and again. You'll end up with something totally different than what you started with.

Pro Tip #2: As a general synthesis guideline, granular synthesis is great for pads and drone-like effects, FM synthesis for synthetic drums, basses and keys, and wavetable synthesis for almost any kind of sound you could imagine, such as cutting leads, pads and basses.

Chapter 2 Sound Design

08 CREATE NEW SAMPLES FROM THE OLD

Transforming old samples to totally new and fresh is possible – with a few sound design tricks.

You might have a great sample library full of drum hits, effects and melodic or vocal chops, but using the same samples in every track you make will have the effect of all your music sounding the same. There are creative ways to freshen up your samples and give them a totally new sound. Some of the techniques include *pitch shifting, formant shifting, bit crushing* and *distortion*. A great commercial pitch and formant shifting plugin is the Little Alterboy by Soundtoys. For your bit crushing duties, grab the free TAL-Bitcrusher. For an unforgiving multiband distortion unit, try the Ohmicide by Ohmforce.

How to: Transform the timbre and character of your samples using Soundtoys Little Alterboy (download the free 30-day fully functional trial at https://www.soundtoys.com/demo/)

1. Insert the Little Alterboy on your desired channel in your DAW.

2. Enable the "Link" –button between the Pitch and Formant –knobs.

3. Twist the Pitch –knob to find a new pitch and timbre for your sample.

4. Use the Formant –knob to further change the timbre of the sound.

Pro Tip #1: Use effects as 100% wet on your mixer channels – this will enable only the pure output of the effect. This could be done with reverbs and delays, among others. The original signal will be instantly transformed to a new one.

Pro Tip #2: Layer samples on top of each other to form a whole new sound. Then bounce the sound to disk, re-import it back to your DAW and apply further processing to make the sample totally unrecognizable.

Chapter 2 Sound Design

Squeeze the most out of creative plugins. Choose only one plugin per category to maximize their effect.

When doing sound design, having multiple plugins that are similar can be a blessing or a curse. When you have four different reverbs, you keep on circling through them to achieve what you are imagining in your head. Instead of wasting time going back and forth between all of them, use only one reverb and tweak it until you get the sound you want. You'll learn plugins inside and out by sticking to one plugin per category (one reverb, delay, distortion, etc.) and ultimately become so much faster and task-oriented in sound design. Not only will you truly *learn* the plugins you choose, but will start to understand better how specific plugins work.

It's worth to mention that other plugins in the same category are surprisingly similar – when you learn to use one with skill, you'll know how to navigate the rest. Also, when working with a single delay for example, you'll end up squeezing sounds out of it you didn't think was possible before. So don't fall into the beginner's trap of using multiple similar plugins at once – you'll never really learn any of them which will hurt your progression as a sound designer.

Pro Tip: Uninstall or delete all but the necessary plugins – force yourself to use only certain ones. Even better, stick to DAW default plugins only, and don't use any third party ones until you have learned to use the DAW plugins skillfully.

Chapter 2 Sound Design

10 Browse Through Old Projects

You'd be surprised how much good sound design you can find in your old projects by going through them.

When you start a new project, you might find yourself in the "blank slate" –situation. This is especially true when figuring out plugin chains to get the right kind of sounds, or creating new sounds completely. The right answers you seek could be found in your older projects, where you have already done the work, finding excellent sound design, mixing and plugin chain decisions. So take a notepad and pen in front of you and carefully go through your past projects while analyzing your favorite sounds in them – and how you got them to sound like it! Sometimes the answers are closer than you think…

How to: Make a list gathering together the best bits of sound design and mixing decisions used in your earlier projects

1. What kind of effects and plugins did you use on drums?

2. How did you use reverbs, delays and other effects?

3. How did you make your synth sounds and why are they sounding so good?

4. How many different sounds did you use to create a certain feeling or vibe in the track?

5. How did you layer different elements to create a cohesive whole?

6. Which synths and plugins did you use over and over again in the project?

7. What was the most radical way you transformed an original sound to create something that sounded fresh and new?

Pro Tip #1: Save all synthesizer sounds as presets for yourself so you can use them in later projects and make modifications to them.

Pro Tip #2: To create your own sound, you need to stay consistent with certain techniques you use in music production. Keep on the lookout for these techniques in older projects and reproduce them in the newer ones to maintain a sound of your own, always taking them a step further.

Chapter 2 Sound Design

CHAPTER 3 – ARRANGEMENT

Study great music – they usually have great arrangements you can learn a lot from.

Simply listening to your favorite music will have an unconscious effect on you. You will start to understand how music is arranged, how intros and outros are made as well as breakdowns, verses and choruses. Over time, you'll build a mental "scaffold" for yourself in terms of music structure, and start to replicate that raw form of arrangement in your own music. Naturally, in order to advance in arrangement, you'll need to constantly keep on making music – while enjoying your favorite artists' music on a daily basis. You should have a pen and paper or digital notepad open when you want to learn from the music made by the pros. You can then easily apply the arrangement tricks to your own music.

How to: Study an arrangement of a track

1. Take note how many *bars* different sections of the track last, such as an intro, verse, chorus and breakdown.

2. Listen what kind of instruments are added as the song progresses, and when.

3. Listen how climaxes are made at different parts, such as right before a chorus and take note what elements were used to create it.

4. Take note how many minutes the track is of length.

5. What are the most dominant elements of the track that keep the music together and how often are they audible?

6. How does the music utilize *rests*?

Pro Tip: Use your favorite piece of music as a reference of arrangement and shamelessly copy the entire arrangement into your own song. Now don't worry – you won't be copying the music which would result in plagiarism, solely the arrangement. You'll still include your own creative twists to it. By doing this you'll gain a tremendous amount of learning – expect a few "a-ha" –moments!

Chapter 3 Arrangement

Create an 8-bar loop representing the full energy of the music.

The smart approach to arrangement is to create a working *loop* first which can then be re-arranged in different ways during the arrangement phase. The point of this method is to create an 8-bar (4 bars work too) loop which represents the peak moment in the music, such as the chorus. When arranging, you can use the loop you made, mute certain instruments from it and gradually introduce them while the track progresses. For example, you could start the track with drums only to introduce the groove, and then bring in the bass and some melodic instruments and finally release the main melody in the breakdown and chorus. This way, you don't have to think about what kind of instruments to add to your track while you build it because they already exist. All you need to do is have fun actually arranging your track and not worry about creating new instruments.

How to: Create a loop with all necessary layers

1. Make sure you have all important drums covered: kick, snare (or clap), hi-hat, crash and toms (or other percussive low-mid element).

2. Have your bass sound working well with the kick drum, forming a solid low end for your music. Choose the bass sound to complement the sound of the kick.

3. Play chords to form the harmonic foundation for you music with instruments such as a piano, guitar or synthesizer keys or pad.

4. Have a lead instrument to introduce a lead melody, such as a synth sound or a vocal – or both.

5. Make sure you have at least one "impact" –effect to start parts of the track with and divide the music into clear sections. The crash cymbal in the drums works well for this, or a white noise sweep. You should play the effect every 8 or 16 bars to introduce a sense of continuity to the music.

6. Make supporting instruments for your main song elements. These could be light melodies, drum grooves or occasional chord stabs that revolve around the main themes of the track.

Pro Tip: When you are finished creating the loop, mix all channels until they sound great. When your track already sounds banging before you start to arrange it, you'll have greater fun arranging it. Basically, stick to EQ, compression and reverb and/or delay and you'll be off to a great start.

Chapter 3 Arrangement

13 ARRANGEMENT AS AN INSTRUMENT

Arrangement is just as creative a process as playing an instrument – you'll need to "play" it too.

By using your great-sounding loop (see Tip #12), duplicate your loop so you'll get a few minutes of playtime with it, and mute all channels and instruments within that loop. Now, play with the mute buttons on the mixer to turn channels on and off. By doing this, you'll stumble upon grooves and instrument combinations you might not have previously thought of while creating the loop, already being accustomed to the sound and groove of it. In a sense, you are playing your own track live while arranging it. Use the feeling of live performance to your advantage and just have a jam with the loop you made and see what comes out of it. At some point, you'll end up with a great drum groove to form a basis to your song, as well as the combinations of main melodic instruments that need to play together. Sometimes a track can have too many (even unnecessary) elements playing at the same time which clogs the music, which makes this method useful for tackling the problem.

How to: "Play" your loop for great arrangement

1. Assuming you have duplicated your loop enough on the DAW timeline and muted all instruments, let's get started.

2. Unmute the kick drum. It's easy to start forming the track around the kick drum.

3. Experiment with unmuting different drum channels, and see which ones work together best and feel right. When you have achieved a great groove, have it play for 8 or 16 bars, until introducing more instruments.

4. See if your 8 or 16 bar groove needs other instruments together with it, such as harmonic or melodic ones. If not, introduce them later on at the 8 or 16 bar mark.

5. Continue to build your track in this manner, arranging the whole track until it is finished, creating build-ups, climaxes, relaxing and peak moments.

Chapter 3 Arrangement

Pro Tip #1: Always introduce something new every 8 or 16 bars, depending how often you feel your music needs them. This way you'll keep your music evolving and not boring. You could always introduce something new at faster intervals, such as 4 bars, depending on the type of song.

Pro Tip #2: Remember that contrast is important in arrangement. When you have achieved a peak moment, it's a good idea to slow the pace a bit. For example: you could build and build the track as it increases in energy, and then suddenly stop the motion by introducing a small break or rest – which introduces a striking contrast. The listeners love contrast in music.

14 PERSPECTIVES FOR ARRANGEMENT

The arrangement methods suggested in this book approach arrangement with different logic but are equally effective.

The first method of arrangement is to start from the beginning, building the track in a chronological order. The second method is to use a full musical loop (Tip #12), such as a chorus, and build the rest around that. You can also use the live performance point of view explained in Tip #12 to arrange your music. They are all great methods of arrangement, ultimately bringing the choice down to personal preference. The start-from-scratch –method is great for producers who can visualize their music in a continuing fashion, "seeing" what needs to happen next. The build-around-the-loop –method is ideal for producers who have a great eye for musical parts that should exist around or lead up to the point where the full-blown loop is. If your loop would represent the chorus of your track, you could leave it where it is and build song parts around it. Arrangement is something that all producers will learn to do in their own way, but a certain universal rule applies: you will need to *build* your track no matter what – and how you decide to build it comes down to your own logic and workflow.

Chapter 3 Arrangement

Pro Tip #1: If you start arranging from the beginning, try to experiment with different styles of starting the track, such as creating a slow, evolving intro with no drums or anticipating and driving intro with a full-on drum groove.

Pro Tip #2: Use volume fades to slowly introduce new instruments, in a stealthy manner. You could also get similar and even more interesting results by filter automation, using a low pass filter to slowly introduce a sound, starting dull and ending up bright.

15 Be Quick with Arrangement

Aim to arrange your track in one music-making session.

When you have all your instruments and loops ready-made, make sure to devote one whole session to arrangement only. In that session, you'll need to lay down the whole rough arrangement of your track, so you'll have all the sections of the song clearly organized – the intro, the verses, choruses, breakdowns, etc. Just like when writing a song, you'd want to lay down the chord structure and main melodies in a short amount of time, you'll want to do the exact same thing with arrangement – put it down quickly because ideas don't last forever. The arrangement of a track is a highly creative process which needs to be treated like one, and not some kind of boring necessity that a piece of music needs. Decide to arrange your track in just one music-making session, and you'll be surprised it can be done in 30 minutes to a few hours. You can always fine-tune little details in arrangement later on, but just have the song frames done quickly.

Chapter 3 Arrangement

If you don't arrange in a swift manner, you could find yourself in the position of not knowing where to take the music at all – and if this happens, try saving your track as a different file and totally re-arrange it from scratch using the method stated here. The point of getting the rough arrangement on lock as fast as possible is that you'll not only visualize your track better in order to "fill in the blanks" later, but create a greater arrangement trusting a moment's gut feeling and emotion. So feel free to turn up the volume and become one with the vibe of your track as you arrange it!

Pro Tip #1: Use the timeline markers in your DAW to divide your track into sections. This helps you visualize your track and work more quickly when arranging. For example: in the very beginning you'd want to create a marker that says "Intro" and when you get to the verse from that point, you'd want to insert a marker there saying "Verse". You'll thank yourself for the easy navigation of large music projects.

Pro Tip #2: Arrange your music in an intimate, private atmosphere. If you get distracted arranging, you could lose the sense of direction where the track needs to go.

CHAPTER 4 – SONGWRITING

16 WRITE WITH INSPIRING INSTRUMENTS

Start the songwriting process with instruments that inspire you and spark creativity.

Before you start writing anything, gather together some of your favorite instruments. These could include traditional instruments such as a piano or guitar, or electronic instruments such as synthesizers, samplers and plugins. The instruments you write music with don't necessarily need to be familiar to you as long as they inspire you, which is the most important thing in writing music. It is also worth noting that different instruments result in different musical outcomes. If you decide to write a song using an ethereal synth pad, the result and feel would be totally different from using an acoustic guitar. You might enjoy playing a piano on your MIDI keyboard, or playing a bassline from a synth over a basic drum groove. One perspective is to think what kind of song you want to write and choose the instruments accordingly. The other way would be to let the instruments lead you into writing certain kind of music. It's your choice. As long as you really enjoy the instruments you make music with, you'll make good music.

Chapter 4 Songwriting

Pro Tip #1: When using synthesizers, browse through the (hundreds of) presets in them to find a sound you like to spark your songwriting process.

Pro Tip #2: Use effect plugins to enhance your favorite instruments even more. Try effects such as chorus, phaser, flanger, reverb and delay for this.

17 S̲ɪɴɢʟᴇ C̲ʜᴏʀᴅ J̲ᴀᴍ

Writing around one chord can be a ton of fun – and easy.

The single chord songwriting method is handy for electronic music producers, especially in the genres of techno, house and other dance music because it lets you jam around the chord without needing to pay attention to creating a (complex) chord progression. Producing a track around one chord will also bring out the *modal* aspect of music, which is desired to create a specific feeling for the track. A synth pad is great for this task, making the single chord feel evolving and rich. If you later decide to create a deeper chord progression for your track, you can use the first solo chord as the *tonal center* for your music to which you can always return to and achieve a sense of rest and fulfillment in your chord progressions. Try regular *triads*, *seventh chords* and *ninth chords*, both *major* and *minor* to find the right kind of energy for your chord.

Pro Tip #1: Try different chord inversions to spice up the chord even more and tweak the sound a bit.

Pro Tip #2: Layer different instruments on top of each other, playing different notes of the same chord, resulting in a more vibrant outcome. For example, let the bass play the tonic note, the synth pad playing the seventh chord without the tonic note and a violin playing the ninth note, forming a ninth chord in total.

Chapter 4 Songwriting

18 WRITING 4 OR 8-BAR CHORD PROGRESSIONS

Figure out a short 4 or 8 bar chord progression to lay down the harmonic foundation for your music.

By creating a *chord progression* lasting 4 or 8 bars, you'll create a set of certain musical rules. It's easy to create melodies around the chord progression you have made because you know what the chords already are, and can use the notes included in the chords and their *scales* to create melodies without needing to wonder where to start. To create a working chord progression, you'll need a tonic chord (see Tip #17). You'll then create the rest of the chords leading away from – and returning back to the tonic for a full emotional circle. The western *diatonic music scale* consists of seven different pitches which can each be used to create a different chord included in the scale.

Because the scale of C major consists of the notes of: c, d, e, f, g, a, b, the C-chord (I) is already the tonic chord, which leaves us with the following chords: D minor (ii), E minor (iii), F major (IV), G major (V), A minor (vi) and B diminished (vii°). You can use the remaining chords to create a progression around the I chord.

How to: Create a chord progression using some popular chord progression formulas as a starting point (let's use C major and A minor as the scales)

1. In a minor scale, try i-VII-VI (A minor-G major-F major). This is a very popular chord progression used in pop, rock and dance music.

2. In a major scale, try I-iii-IV-V (C major-E minor-F major-G major). This is a happy but melancholic chord progression.

3. In a minor scale, try VI-VII-v-VI (F major-G major-E minor-F major). This progression would work great in a chorus and has certain tension to it.

4. In a major scale, try IV-vi-V-ii (F major-A minor-G major-D minor). This is a very stylish and modern chord progression which would work well in an emotional electronic music track.

Chapter 4 Songwriting

Pro Tip #1: Write a looping chord progression, where the last chord feels like it needs to go back to the first chord, achieving a sense of fulfillment.

*Pro Tip #2: The chord formula for the **major scale** is: I ii iii IV V vi vii° and the **minor scale**: i ii° III iv v VI VII. They are written in roman numerals, where the upper-case letters indicate major chords and the lower-case letters minor chords. The small circle means that the chord is diminished. You can use these formulas when you create your chord progressions.*

19 WRITE DOWN SONG TITLES FIRST

Have ready-made titles for tracks that you are about to write.

If you have already created the titles for your music, it's easier to dive into the songwriting process, because you have a specific goal in mind. For example, if you choose to make a track for the title "Midnight", you would specifically aim for the kind of vibe the title suggests. So instead of always leaving the titling as the last step in the music creation process, make it the first step instead. Your songwriting will thank you. In fact, the music you make will be more focused and on point. Try to write a title or two down every day, until you have a large list to choose titles from. Whenever you decide to start producing a new track, just look through the titles and see what you happen to feel like at that moment. Naturally, delete any used titles from your list to keep it organized.

Pro Tip #1: Always write down titles on your phone or notepad, wherever you are. It's easier to come up with great titles when you are on the move or experiencing something in your life.

Pro Tip #2: Problems with creating a theme for an album? No problem, just write down a handful of titles about a certain subject — at least 10. If you stick to creating your music around these titles, it will ensure your album sounds cohesive having a theme and not like a random collection of tracks.

Chapter 4 Songwriting

20 ALWAYS RECORD EVERYTHING

Whenever you jam around in your DAW, make sure you're recording.

In the digital era there's no excuse to NOT record since all you'll lose is some hard disk space. There's no expensive tape involved like decades ago. With that said, when you are playing around with your MIDI keyboard or instruments, just arm the specific track to record and off you go. It's easier to take a listen to recorded ideas that just "burst" out of you in the spur of a moment, instead of trying to remember what you just accidentally played. Great music comes from the heart, which is why the record-button is a musician's lifejacket. Even when you are just experimenting or starting to write a song, it's smart to have recording enabled, because often it is the smartest move you can make in songwriting.

Pro Tip #1: If you have created a loop or chord progression, just duplicate it as long as you want in the DAW's timeline so you have enough time to record and jam.

Pro Tip #2: Enable loop recording in your DAW so you can select an area to loop which will record indefinitely until stopped. Loop recording is handy if you want to nail a certain take or part in your track.

Chapter 5 – Motivation

21 Make Honest Music

Whatever you do, make sure the music you make is honest and real.

Don't force yourself to make only certain kind of music. You shouldn't feel pressured about getting your music accepted by peers around you. This will only drain all the creativity out of you. The music you make should flow out of YOU. Listen to yourself, take a good look at the life situations and experiences you are currently going through and try to channel those energies into music – it doesn't matter what kind of music it is. At least it will be honest! By creating what you feel will ensure that your music will always stay real, which is also what the best artists constantly do – put out solid music one tune after another. Could you imagine classics like Queen's *Bohemian Rhapsody* or Michael Jackson's *Billie Jean* making it through the test of time if they weren't honestly and truthfully written pieces of music – not to mention them being totally unique. Your music will never be loved by everyone, but no one can doubt it if it truly mirrors the passion you have devoted to making it.

Chapter 5 Motivation

Pro Tip: If you ever start having second doubts about your own music and feel abandoned surrounded by the masses of popular music, tell yourself that you are doing something right and turn the situation into inspiration. When the time comes to showcase your music to influential people in the music industry, your music will have a better chance surviving than the rest of the "ordinary" tunes. Don't submit to being a sheep — become a wolf instead.

Stay away from "forms" in music – let it build itself naturally.

As an electronic music producer, you might be worried about things such as creating intros and outros that are DJ-friendly, or having a certain kind of arrangement that a specific genre tends to have. While making music, don't worry about these things. As a rule of thumb, if the track is good, the DJ's will still play it and the people will still listen to it. Just do what you do and let the track form itself. If you feel like the music should begin from total silence, slowly fading into a majestic chorus, feel free to do so and don't ruin the beginning by creating an unmotivating intro that you don't want to include in it. Parts like DJ-friendly intros and outros can always be added later on if necessary. If the music is great, the crowd will demand the DJ to play it, no matter the form of the music. Get it? Make your music with feeling – not shackling it to a certain form.

Pro Tip #1: Stay innovative – the freshest tracks are usually the ones with the most unusual forms, arrangements, progressions and moments of impact.

Pro Tip #2: Always try to include something new in your music. Even if you decide to use generic grooves, chord progressions and melodies, try to execute them in an interesting manner using neat-sounding samples or unorthodox instrumentation.

Chapter 5 Motivation

23 GET OUT OF YOUR COMFORT ZONE

Every once in a while, do things differently from the usual safe methods.

While being a rather cliché, getting out of your comfort zone is necessary in making music and progressing in it. A great example would be choosing a new time signature for your next track: if you're used to making music in 4/4, which is the regular time signature for pop, rock and dance music, try to write a track in 6/8 or ¾ and see what comes out of it. You might be surprised (and even learn something new!) Doing things in a radically different way can be an eye-opening experience and a fresh channel of inspiration for making music. Just like in life, you need to step out of the bubble every once in a while and challenge yourself to succeed – the same applies to music.

Pro Tip #1: Challenge yourself to create one new track from scratch by using a whole new DAW. This forces you to think differently and revives your creative brain from the constant "hibernation" that routine causes. For music producers and mixers, learning a new DAW equals richness of experience.

Pro Tip #2: Challenge yourself to create a track where you design all sounds from scratch and don't use any ready-made samples or instruments. You could make all drums, melodic and harmonic instruments using a synthesizer, for example. Or you could record a part of your sounds with microphones. Enrich your knowledge and competence by stepping out of the comfort zone!

Chapter 5 Motivation

Form friendships with fellow producers and musicians.

Get together and stay in contact with your music producer friends – they are your #1 source for staying motivated in music. If you are alone with your music for long periods of time, things can get very hard after a while, even to the point of depression and lack of motivation. Think of your music production friends as your personal safety net you can always "fall" on. If you don't have real life producer friends or don't have the chance to get to know some people involved in music, join an online community such as a music forum or Facebook group. Have discussions about music, personal struggles and experiences. When these issues are shared, you don't feel that you are alone anymore, which in itself is a great motivational boost for making music. Have people listen to your music, listen to other people's music and exchange constructive feedback with each other – it's healthy to learn about another musician's creative process while getting a fresh pair of ears to listen to your tracks. In the process, you'll grow as a music producer and musician.

Pro Tip #1: Exchange *music production secrets, sample libraries, sounds and plugins. You can only gain from other producers' experience – and vice versa.*

Pro Tip #2: Make *real-life collaborations happen and spend nights together with other producers. These situations are golden for any music producer, acting as atmospheres of true innovation and creativity.*

Chapter 5 Motivation

Accept the fact that sometimes music just doesn't happen.

Big part of the artistic circulation is not being able to make music – it's better to just accept it. Sometimes, the stars just aren't aligned for making music, which is okay. It's important to show up for music making sessions on a daily or weekly basis, but it won't always be ideal and inspirational. You won't always create satisfying music or even anything at all. To tackle the issue, it's best to do something else with your spare time, such as devote time to other hobbies and activities. By doing something else for a while, preferably away from the studio, you'll be surprised how the mind clarifies itself while regaining inspiration for music. The important thing is not to force making music, because great music can't possibly happen in that confusing, emotional state. If you're a true artist, learn to embrace the times when you can't make music – take these times as signs instead to point your creative energies elsewhere for a while.

Pro Tip #1: Do something useful with your music making time, such as reorganizing your sample libraries, sound design, cleaning and color-coding your projects or analyzing your old projects and mixes for useful plugin chains.

Pro Tip #2: Play an instrument. Don't think about making music, just play and have fun. Find a backing track of your favorite song on YouTube and have a jam with an instrument over it. Your musical energies will replenish when you simply become one with the music.

Chapter 5 Motivation

HEY, I HOPE YOU ENJOYED THIS BOOK. CHECK OUT MY OTHER BOOKS TO SUPPORT YOU IN MAKING MUSIC AND STAY ON TOP OF YOUR MUSIC PRODUCTION GAME...

-Roy Wilkenfeld

Electronic Music: 25 Mixing Tips for Modern Electronic Music Production

Music Theory: Simple Music Theory for Electronic Music Production: Beginner's Guide to Rhythm, Chords, Scales and a lot, lot more...

THANK YOU FOR READING THIS BOOK

Please check out the Production Wisdom blog for more great tips and information about mixing, music production, techniques and philosophy.

productionwisdom.com

Made in the USA
Lexington, KY
30 April 2017